WATCH YOUR MOUTH

WATCH YOUR MOUTH

Engaging and Releasing the Creative Power of the Tongue

EDDIE JAMES

Largo, MD

ISBN 9781562295257
Christian Living Books, Inc.
P.O. Box 7584
Largo, MD 20792
christianlivingbooks.com
We bring your dreams to fruition.

CONTENTS

INTRODUCTION

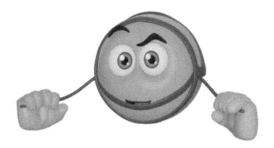

The creative power of the tongue transcends the natural into the supernatural. At creation, God ordained us to heal or kill, shape or destroy, bind or loose. He allows us to make our own choices. We choose how we use our words and what decisions we make.

The creative power of words makes all of us superhuman as we resemble God who "calls those things that be not as though they were" (Romans 4:17). However, many people are ignorant of the power which is resident in their tongues.

Wars, crimes, and atrocities are consequences of abusing the tongue's power. Indeed, many wars have been fought because world leaders didn't know when to speak with tact and wisdom. Alas, millions of people have died because men spoke words of hate and anarchy.

> *Death and life are in the power of the tongue: and they*
> *that love it shall eat the fruit thereof.* (Proverbs 18:21)

The fruit of life and death can be produced by the tongue. The psalmist understood this potential:

I will take heed to my ways that I sin not with my tongue:
I will keep my mouth with a bridle, while the wicked is
before me. (Psalm 39:1)

What harvest would you like to reap from your tongue? Life or death? Do you often feel you are not fully utilizing the power of your tongue? Do you want to develop the ability to create things out of nothing? Then, you have the right book in your hands.

Watch Your Mouth is a 40-day encounter with God that unveils fresh revelations about maximizing the full potential of your tongue. Do you want to live your best life and be the best version of yourself? Then this book is your one-way-ticket to all the Lord has for you.

FROWARD MOUTH

Put away from thee a froward mouth, and perverse lips put far from thee. (Proverbs 4:24)

Froward means distortion, crookedness, or deviation from the standard. It appears many times in the scriptures, though not many people understand the word. Now, if froward means deviation from the standard, what then is the standard?

Words are powerful; they shape our lives and define our destinies. The Bible reveals that our words must always line up with God's Word, which is the standard that calibrates the right words (Isaiah 8:20). We must train our mouths to utter words of life.

A froward mouth is an abuse—abnormal use of the tongue. The Word of God encourages us to be positive, but the froward think and speak negatively. The Word of God urges us not to give up, but the froward tells himself, "I can't succeed. Let me quit." Our lives proceed in the direction of the most dominant words and prevalent thoughts.

Froward mouths speak everything other than the Word of God, which is life in abundance. My friend, put away your froward mouth. Embrace the Word of Truth. Speak powerful words that bring life to any dead situation. Don't give in to the whispers of the enemy. Remember, Satan is the father of lies (John 8:44). Attune your heart to God's holy standards. Use your princely privilege to change your circumstances.

> ## PRAYER
>
> *Father, I recognize that I have been froward with my mouth and attitude. I'm asking for Your mercy and forgiveness as I repent for all of it. I now commit and dedicate my mouth to You. Please use it as a tool and instrument to uplift, instruct, and heal for kingdom advancement and the fulfillment of Your will. I further ask You to empower my mouth to always speak that which will glorify You and bring honor to Your name. In Jesus' name I pray. Amen.*

ENSNARED BY HIS WORD

Thou art snared with the words of thy mouth, thou art taken with the words of thy mouth. (Proverbs 6:2)

The book of 2 Samuel opens with a tragic event: the death of King Saul and his son, Jonathan. It was a terrible day of mourning for David, whose honor for the Lord's anointed was profound. Not only that; it also features the story of a young talebearer whose mouth got him into terrible trouble. Seeking David's favor, he claimed to have killed Saul since David was positioned to be the next king. He thought that news would please David. He was wrong.

David said unto him, Thy blood be upon thy head; for thy mouth hath testified against thee, saying, I have slain the Lord's anointed. (2 Samuel 1:16)

This guy didn't realize how much David revered Saul and was ready to preserve his respect for Saul even in his death. Now, think about when your words almost or, in fact, led you straight into a trap.

How often do you utter statements that create obstacles instead of gateways of blessings? The devil doesn't automatically gain a foothold in your life. But this unrelenting enemy seeks to take away your freedom by looking for loopholes created by your words. He longs to see you make nets around your situation instead of hope. He then capitalizes on this weakness to attack you.

Here's my counsel to you, dear reader: choose your words carefully and *Stand fast therefore in the liberty wherewith Christ hath made us free and be not entangled again with the yoke of bondage* (Galatians 5:1).

PRAYER

Dear Lord, enlightened by Your Word today, I acknowledge that negative words can derail and destroy my destiny. Therefore, I repent from every word and statement I have ever made that has ensnared me in any shape or form. Colossians 2:14 says that You've blotted out the ordinances that condemned me. Therefore, through the blood of Jesus, I revoke, cancel and nullify any negative statement and words I have ever spoken to my disadvantage. By the blood of Jesus, let any evil consequences from those words be overturned and averted. Father, please "Set a guard over my mouth, LORD; keep watch over the door of my lips" and teach me to speak out of wisdom. In Jesus' name I pray. Amen.

HONEYCOMB LIPS

*For the lips of a strange woman drop as an honeycomb,
and her mouth is smoother than oil.* (Proverbs 5:3)

If the honeycomb is compared to human lips, it means words can be irresistible. That's an accurate description of the strange woman in the text above. Though the Bible is highlighting women in this particular scripture, it's just as true for men who would intentionally lead you astray. Seducers have an uncanny ability to allure and distract anyone who listens to the words that drip like honey from their lips. Moreover, King Solomon advises young people to beware of such malicious wolves in sheep's clothing.

You were put here for a purpose. Maximize your potential. Accomplish all that you were destined for. Apply the wisdom of the Word and keep your feet from the door of the strange woman. By her words, she will entice you and bring you into untold calamity.

The scriptures add that the reason for her flatteries is to destroy her prey as a lion tears apart a sheep. However, the Bible says…

> *But her end is bitter as wormwood, sharp as a two-edged sword.* (Proverbs 5:4)

This scene underscores the power of words. This woman is smart. She knows what she is doing. She possesses one of the most dangerous weapons on Earth—words.

The adversary subtly enters our lives by any means necessary. Expect some juicy enticements from him. That's his nature. But you can defuse the enemy's bomb by taking heed to Solomon's advice:

> *That thou mayest regard discretion, and that thy lips may keep knowledge.* (Proverbs 5:2)

Be rooted in Jesus and filled with His wisdom. This keeps you from the antics of the seducer. May you be preserved to fulfill your purpose on this earth.

PRAYER

Lord, I employ divine understanding and discernment to locate any honeycomb lips that lead to the destruction of my destiny. Lord, keep me from any deceitful personality on assignment to use seduction to entrap my soul. Grant me the grace and the anointing of Joseph to flee from all such devices and schemes. Thank You, Lord, for causing me to run through every troop and leap over every wall. I declare that I am an overcomer in Jesus' name. Amen.

SIN OF THE MOUTH

For the sin of their mouth and the words of their lips let them even be taken in their pride: and for cursing and lying which they speak. (Psalm 59:12)

I n context, David pronounced judgment on his enemies who sought to destroy him. He provided a reason why God should vindicate him and eliminate them. Guess what the reason was? For the sin of their mouths.

That poignant factor demands our attention. Just as the psalmist accused his enemies based on the nature of their words, the adversary, the devil, can also make grievous accusations against us if we do not use our mouths wisely.

Don't use foul or abusive language. Let everything
you say be good and helpful, so that your words will
be an encouragement to those who hear them.

(Ephesians 4:29, NLT)

Spewing out words of reproach and malice is as deadly as piercing someone with a sword. Speaking nothing but evil shows that pride is not far away. Whatever is not of God should not proceed from your mouth. Using curse words, for instance, can be as disgusting to God as rolling in the mud.

The sin of the mouth is unpleasant to God. It defies nature and liquidates everything good in a believer. What fruit do you have on your lips? Blessings or curses? Lies or truth? Choose blessings; choose truth so you and your house may live evermore in God's presence.

PRAYER

Dear Lord, please help me to revere You in the way that I speak. Cause me to not trivialize the sin of the mouth. Like Job covenanted with his eyes not to look lustfully at a woman so do I commit my mouth to bless only and not to curse, honoring God and blessing humanity. Like the pen of a ready writer, so instruct my tongue to inscribe the creative epistles of life on individuals, families, and people. Help me to always be mindful, this I pray with thanksgiving, in Jesus' name. Amen.

NAUGHTY PERSON

A naughty person, a wicked man, walketh with a fro-ward mouth. (Proverbs 6:12)

I n his Bible commentary, John Gill describes a naughty and wicked person as "a man of iniquity." Iniquity is when a person continues to do something that is not good. Iniquity is not the same as making a mistake or missing the mark. Iniquity implies willful, continual, habitual sin. A naughty person works outside of God's plan with no regard for the integrity of His Word.

> *Let me describe for you a worthless and a wicked man;*
> *first, he is a constant liar.* (Proverbs 6:12, TLB)

The Living Bible defines the word "naughty" as worthless, one who has almost nothing to offer, devoid of valuable substance but rich in lies and deception. He spurts out blasphemy against God. In the claim of his wisdom, his ignorance and foolishness will be revealed.

Moreover, a naughty person is best identified by his nasty mouth. No matter how distinguished you may be in society, if you do not maintain wholesome conversation, it's a clear manifestation of naughtiness. A naughty person turns away from God to his sin. Nevertheless, God never turns His back on us.

It is so much better to be thoughtful than to be vulgar. Choose to use your words to build and not to destroy. As you speak by divine inspiration that transcends every form of carnality, you will find favor.

From this point forward, speak useful and truthful words so you can be valuable to yourself, mankind, and ultimately to God.

PRAYER

Elohim, I thank You for Your Word which is quick, sharp and useful for instruction, doctrine, correction, and training in righteousness. Lord, through Your Word, I have discovered naughty ways in me. I therefore ask You to enable me to pursue You passionately until I am changed and totally transformed. From this point forward, may I speak by divine inspiration that transcends every form of carnality in me. By the enablement of the Holy Spirit, I will speak useful, truthful, constructive and empowering words so that I can be valuable to God, mankind, and myself. In Jesus' name I pray. Amen.

WORDS LIKE SWORDS

The words of his mouth were smoother than butter,
but war was in his heart: his words were softer than
oil, yet were they drawn swords. (Psalm 55:21)

The mystery of double-identity is wrapped up in hypocrisy with a side order of upheaval. It is a common feature of those whose nature is contrary to the nature of the living God. Hypocrisy was common among the Pharisees. They taught people the law; yet they made false accusations against Jesus Christ.

> *Who whet their tongue like a sword, and bend their*
> *bows to shoot their arrows, even bitter words.*
>
> (Psalm 64:3)

We must realize that our words reveal the spiritual condition of our hearts. This is a reality. However, there are enemies like friends, killers like supporters, and destroyers like helpers who utter words opposite of their intentions. Beware of the softness of their speech and gentleness in their actions. Cruel intentions may be just beneath the surface.

This was the case with King David. Enemies in friend's clothing surrounded him. However, by divine discernment, he could identify them. You do not have to live in fear and suspicion. God will protect and keep you from sword-tongued people whose words sound "smoother than oil."

Also, keep your heart and mouth in tune. Be sure that you mean what you say and only say what you mean. That's a divine attribute of the child of God. May the Lord give you the grace to stay upright in words and actions.

PRAYER

Dear Lord, Your Word says that You desire truth in my innermost being. May Christ, who is the truth, finds practical expression in all my dealings. Please help me not to be a dual personality with a double tongue. I pray that my "yes" will be "yes" and my "no" be "no". May I never be found criticizing nor slandering people behind their backs while putting on a different front before their faces. I ask, Lord, to be delivered from deceitful people, any wolf in sheep's clothing, or any disguised agent from Hell. Please activate my spiritual senses to always walk in spiritual intelligence. In Jesus' name I pray. Amen.

KEEP YOUR LIFE

*He that keepeth his mouth keepeth his life: but he
that openeth wide his lips shall have destruction.*

(Proverbs 13:3)

The book of Nehemiah aptly describes the spiritual strategy we
must employ. Nehemiah built the city walls and installed gates
to prevent unauthorized access into the city. Without the gates, his
efforts would have been wasted; enemies would attack and again
bring down the walls.

The heart has some access gates. And the quality of a man's life
is as good as the stuff he allows into and out of his heart. The verse
above offers a strong warning that underscores the fact that destruction follows those who have no filters on their mouths.

There are words to be kept secret and words to share with family and friends. Carelessly unleashing the contents of your thoughts can cause severe problems to you or another person.

> *Those who control their tongue will have a long life;*
> *opening your mouth can ruin everything.*
> (Proverbs 13:3, NLT)

The young man in 2 Samuel 1, lost control of his tongue and paid severely for it. His sun set in its prime because he had no filter and could not control his tongue.

Words are powerful! They hold in themselves both life and death for the speaker, depending on what was said, as well as when and how it was expressed. Shut the gates of your mouth. Keep your life.

PRAYER

Lord, Your Word says that "If any of You lack wisdom, let Him ask the Lord who gives generously to all without finding fault, and it will be given to You." Today, I ask for Your kind of wisdom to enable me to use my tongue wisely. Please grant me the ability to bridle my tongue and the grace to exercise restraint. Oh Lord, I pray that I may not ruin my life or that of others because of ignorance. In Jesus' name I pray. Amen.

WHAT ARE YOUR INTENTIONS?

They only consult to cast him down from his Excellency: they delight in lies: they bless with their mouth, but they curse inwardly. Selah. (Psalm 62:4)

Psalm 62 is a heartfelt prayer of protection written by David. He was attacked verbally, and all sorts of propaganda put his life on the line. David's enemies, persecutors, and slanderers gave him so much trouble that he had to commit himself entirely to God for protection.

The Hebrew word for "excellency" is *s'eth* meaning an exalted position, dignity, loftiness, and uprising. David's antagonists connived to discourage him from looking unto God, his fortress, and rock. They sought to lower him from his privileged position in God to a demeaning, low position.

That is how destructive the tongue can be. It can depress someone so much that death seems a better option. Of course, that is when the tongue is misused.

How do you use your tongue at home, work, and everywhere you go? Does the thought of a promoted colleague make you so green with envy that you say all kinds of negative words just to pull them down? Do you whisper derogatory remarks about them to ruin reputations and shift people's attention to you?

> You talk in good line, but every blessing breathes a curse. (Psalm 62:4, TLB)

What exactly are your intentions? How glorious it would be if we adapt our tongues to the ways of the Lord and speak when and how He wants us to.

PRAYER

Lord, I thank You for this day. Please deliver me from the lashing of the tongue of evil men and evil forces. May I not be an evil tongue targeted toward the downfall of people. May my tongue be used to uplift people and to keep them lifted. May I not contribute or support the destruction of another. Use my tongue for positive influence. In Jesus' name I pray. Amen.

STRANGE CHILDREN

Rid me, and deliver me from the hand of strange children, whose mouth speaketh vanity, and their right hand is a right hand of falsehood. (Psalm 144:11)

S trange children are everywhere. They aim to destroy others with their tongues and speak all manner of lies to slander their neighbors.

Strange children, according to the psalmist, describes the descendants of the Moabites, Edomites, and Hittites, to name a few. Vulgarity, vanity, and profanity are a few of their characteristics.

> *Rescue me and deliver me from the control of foreigners, whose mouths speak lies, and whose right hand deceives.* (Psalm 144:11, ISV)

Like David prayed in the above scripture, may we not fall victim to the hands of strange individuals whose attitudes can be mistaken for kindness when they intend hate.

Dear reader, if you are in Christ Jesus, you are a new creature. Live like God—your heavenly Father. Do away with all forms of evil from your life. And keep your mouth from speaking vanity.

God bless you.

PRAYER

Father, deliver me from the hand of strange children, whose mouth speaks vanity, and whose right hand is deceptive. Rescue and deliver me from those whose mean me evil. May I not fall victim to the hands of strange individuals whose attitudes can be mistaken for kindness when they intend hate. Keep my mouth from speaking vanity and let vanity be far from me. In Jesus' name I pray. Amen.

DESTROYER OF NEIGHBORS

An hypocrite with his mouth destroyeth his neighbour:
but through knowledge shall the just be delivered.

(Proverbs 11:9)

Hypocrisy is the mother of slander. The Bible says hypocrites appear to be friends to their neighbors, but in reality, they are backstabbers.

With flattery and deception, they manipulate honest people who are oblivious to their underlying intentions. False teachers of God's Word fall into this category. They teach what they do not practice just like the Pharisees. They preach heresies and cause people to be defiled.

With their words, the godless destroy their friends,
but knowledge will rescue the righteous.

(Proverbs 11:9, NLT)

You must stay full of the knowledge of God's Word. This makes it difficult for anyone to dissuade you from following the truth. Then, you must ensure that your life matches up with your profession; otherwise, you'll be a hypocrite too.

PRAYER

Dear Lord, please protect me from hypocrites who appear to be friends, but in reality, are backstabbers. May I never walk in their path nor entertain their company. Deliver me from fake friends and open my eyes to see those whose friendship is pure and sincere. Help me grow in revelational knowledge of Your will, wisdom, and understanding. Enable me to stand my ground and defend the integrity of the scripture as well my faith in the Lord Jesus. In Jesus' name I pray. Amen.

DAY 11

THE FEAR OF GOD

The fear of the LORD is to hate evil: pride, and arrogancy, and the evil way, and the froward mouth, do I hate. (Proverbs 8:13)

The fear of God is not like the fear one would have of a rattlesnake. Rather, it is devout affection and godly fear toward Him. It can be likened to the fear that exists between a child and his parents. This type of fear is divine because it is consistent with joy, faith, freedom, and absolute dependence on God the Father for everything in life.

The reverent fear and worshipful awe of the Lord [includes] the hatred of evil; pride, arrogance, the

evil way, and perverted and twisted speech I hate.
(Proverbs 8:13, AMPC)

The fear of God results in a life free from evil and perverseness.

The quickest way to show you love and fear God is to hate what He hates—evil. and love what He loves righteousness. It is almost impossible not to identify a perverted tongue with pride and arrogance. These characteristics of evil are detestable to God and should be estranged from us.

We must seek to express a holy fear of God by not uttering perverted words. Are you fond of cursing, using profanity, or even verbal abuse? Manifest God's nature in you by cleaning up your speech.

Stay close to the Spirit of God and allow Him to teach you the fear of God so your conversation will be acceptable, positive, and productive.

PRAYER

Holy Father, I come to You this day with an open heart. Endow me with the Spirit of the fear of the Lord to enable me to walk the way Jesus walked. Let what was present in the life of the holy men of old, be present with me that I will be consistent with their lifestyles. May my life, from this day forward, be a total reflection of You. In Jesus' name I pray. Amen.

BECOMING A WELL OF LIFE

The mouth of a righteous man is a well of life: but violence covereth the mouth of the wicked.

(Proverbs 10:11)

Righteousness is not a function of what you did right. It is a function of what God did right for you in His Son, Jesus Christ. Righteousness is being in right standing with God. You may say, "I'm not worthy" or "I'll never be good enough." Take a minute and think about what Isaiah says:

> *For we have all become like one who is unclean [ceremonially, like a leper], and all our righteousness (our best deeds of rightness and justice) is like filthy rags or a polluted garment; we all fade like a leaf, and our iniquities, like the wind, take us away [far*

from God 's favor, hurrying us toward destruction].
(Isaiah 64:6, AMP)

Having put on Christ, who is our righteousness, the words that proceed from our hearts through our mouths provide clear evidence of our new identity. Like a living fountain that gushes fresh water, so is the mouth of a man who is in right position with God.

The quality of our words is an indication of our walk with God. You cannot commune deeply with God without His holy nature rubbing off on you. Whatever is in your heart will flow out of your mouth. We should speak wholesome, refreshing, and revitalizing words that inspire others to live righteously and encourage them to love God more.

On the other hand, those that are disconnected from God speak wickedness. They cannot help themselves because their hearts are impure. Their words are negative, damaging, and hurtful.

Therefore, maintain your privileged position in Christ Jesus. Stand in His liberty and speak only words that will minister grace to your hearers. Become a living spring from which life flows into others.

PRAYER

Lord, I acknowledge that born again believers are a well full of everlasting water. Therefore, I declare this day that I am a well. May I pour life and light into the lives of people. May I be a true representation of an oasis in the desert places of life. May I flow forth with healing, restoration, and deliverance without restraint. Make me a true blessing through the instrument of my tongue. In Jesus' name I pray. Amen.

DEW OF BLESSINGS

Blessings are upon the head of the just: but violence covereth the mouth of the wicked. (Proverbs 10:6)

As dew distills from the sky and settles on the green, lush field, so do praises and blessings descend upon the man who walks in the light. The just man cares more about his neighbor than himself. He does not seek personal gain. He is not too cynical to reward the deserving. No wonder blessings gravitate to him.

If you're good, heaven recognizes and showers blessings upon you. It does not matter whether you are a leader or follower, preacher or laity, spiritual and physical blessings will follow you as long as you are faithful.

But the speech of the wicked is a cover for violence.
(Proverbs 10:6, DARBY)

People disconnected from God are usually miserable. When they intend to speak peace, they pronounce war. Why? Their hearts are full of violence. They have stuffed their souls with destructive content, so the mouth cannot help but utter negativity and spark contention among folks. Be mindful of how you use your tongue.

Tie your tongue to your walk with God. Stay just; let the blessings of the Lord distill on you like the dew of heaven. Beware of wickedness around you and keep your heart from dwelling on violence. You can mend the broken-hearted by God's Word and neutralize the time bomb waiting to explode in their hearts.

PRAYER

Heavenly Father, grant me the grace to keep my words clearn. I pray to be able to come under the influence of Your blessings. Open my eyes so that I can clearly see any form of wickedness around me. Purify my thoughts so that I never dwell on violence. Please help me guard me heart will all diligence. In Jesus' name I pray. Amen.

STAY OUT
OF TROUBLE

FOOLISHNESS!

A fool's lips enter into contention, and his mouth calleth for strokes. (Proverbs 18:6)

A fool described as a self-confident guy who lives outside of God's ways and directions. He is never gracious or wise. Instead, he is always causing trouble and starting some drama.

Check what reaction your words invoke in your hearers. Are they actions of peace or war?

When the name Adolf Hitler is mentioned, what comes to mind? You remember a man whose words provoked the death of millions of Jews. What about the Rev. Dr. Martin Luther King, Jr.? With words, he led a peaceful movement that inspired presidents and citizens alike to fight for justice and necessary change.

Words are like weapons. If they are wielded by fools, lives will be destroyed. However, if wisely employed, freedom and liberty will come forth.

The fool not only brings pain and hardship to his listeners. He also suffers lots of heartbreak himself. In fact, John Gill's commentaries describe judgment upon the fool for misleading people.

Stay out of trouble. Be wise! Let your words stream down from the throne room of God. They will bring peace, joy, and blessings on your listeners instead of contention.

PRAYER

Lord, thank You for the gift of today. I pray for Your grace that comes through knowledge in the name of Jesus. I pray for the understanding that will deliver me from trouble. Help me to engage the keys that will not only keep me out of trouble but enable me help others to stay out of trouble. May I speak the right words at the right time for the benefit of all and to the glory and praise of Your most holy name. In Jesus' name I pray. Amen.

GETTING RID
OF PRIDE

In the mouth of the foolish is a rod of pride: but the lips of the wise shall preserve them. (Proverbs 14:3)

Who is the LORD that I should obey him and let Israel go? I do not know the LORD, and I will not let Israel go. (Exodus 5:2)

That statement from Exodus is probably one of the proudest made in history. Pharaoh may have thought he was hurling insults at Moses. Unknown to him, he was directly attacking God Almighty. We all know how that ended.

God revealed His mighty power by afflicting Egypt with ten unbearable plagues. Ultimately, both Pharaoh and his armies drowned in the Red Sea. After all, he had asked, *Who is the Lord?* He definitely received an answer to that question!

Only fools pride themselves in their positions at the expense of God's glory. They ask questions only God is entitled to ask. They engage their mouths in foolish discussions. Pharoah's words affected the entire nation. He wasn't just hurting himself.

But those who are wise soak in humility. They realize they are successful by the grace of God. Their lips speak gracefully, and God sanctions their words with the riches of His blessings.

It is imperative to be humble. Words spoken in pride cut in both directions—at the listeners and speakers themselves.

PRAYER

Heavenly Father, let the spirit of humility take a hold of my heart and grant that I will not use my tongue pridefully. Give me the grace to stay humble like Christ my Lord. May any root of pride in my flesh be identified by the Word of God and removed by the power of the Spirit. Help me to always know that it is not by my might, my power, my wisdom, my expertise, my status, my beauty, nor my education, but it is by Your enabling power. In Jesus' name I pray. Amen.

PARALYZED ATHLETE

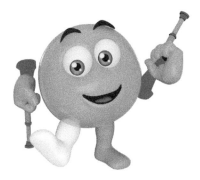

*The legs of the lame are not equal: so is a parable in
the mouth of fools.* (Proverbs 26:7)

Have you ever witnessed a lame man dancing? Not a good look,
right? Due to no fault of the lame guy, his legs betrayed him.
While he intended to lift one leg, the other went up instead. He was
probably kicking somebody on one side and knocking somebody
down on the other.

That is a perfect description of a fool trying to be wise. Because
his life is not consistent with what he says, it is difficult for him to
deliver the right message. Even when he is speaking the truth, there
is usually no substance in his speech.

A fool with words of wisdom is like an athlete with legs that can't move. (Proverbs 26:7, CEV)

Until his words change his identity, no parables from his mouth will impact people.

How is this relevant to us today? You see, you may have the right words, but if you do not know how and when to say them, they are useless. They may even spark arguments or irritate the hearers.

Perhaps, nobody listens to you even when you have something important to say. First, deal with what is in your heart. Present it to God for divine cleansing. Let Him transform your personality! Also, ask Him for guidance. Let the Holy Spirit teach you what to say, how, and when to say it. Let Him be the source and director of your speech. Then, your words will be accepted and honored.

PRAYER

Gracious Lord, I thank You for creating me in Your image and after Your likeness. I ask that You grant me the grace to walk in that understanding. Lord, may who I am in Christ always influence what I say, when I speak, where I speak, and how I speak. Purify my heart with the fire of Your Spirit and enable me to have absolute control over my self-image and speech. I thank You, Lord, for answered prayer. In Jesus' name I pray. Amen.

FREE YOURSELF

A fool's mouth is his destruction, and his lips are the snare of his soul. (Proverbs 18:7)

A world of iniquity resides in the mouth and tongue of a wicked man. Those disconnected from God are full of themselves and the vile content they consume. When they speak, it causes nothing but trouble.

The mouth of a foolish man not only brings punishment upon him, but it also affects others negatively. Those who are quick to curse, pass blame, and fault the system for their failures despise those who take responsibility for their own lives.

Let the Word of Christ dwell in you richly, so that trouble will be far from you. Always be positive and cast down every stronghold of negativity.

The foolish person whose hope and life depend on the fleeting pleasures of the world, does not cease to have issues with other people. His lips ensnare his soul, weaken his conscience, and enslave his body.

> *For by thy words thou shalt be justified, and by thy words, thou shalt be condemned.* (Matthew 12:37)

God is just, kind, and wise. He has put the power to set free and make captive in our tongues. Use your tongue for freedom, not condemnation. Pronounce great things into your own life, and so shall it be.

PRAYER

Dear Father, through the blood of our Lord Jesus Christ, I free myself from any self-inflicted curses and negative consequences emanating from any reckless word I have ever spoken. Grant that I will access the body of knowledge that establishes total freedom and that I will live in complete victory. Lord, You promised in Your Word that calamity will be far from the tent of the righteous. Therefore, keep me from trouble and destruction. In Jesus' name I pray. Amen.

DEVOURING WORDS

Thou lovest all devouring words, O thou deceitful tongue. (Psalm 52:4)

Like a lion preying on a deer, so does the deceitful tongue prey on its victims. A deceitful tongue is capable of destroying lives and even an entire nation.

What type of tongue do you have? Do your words build or destroy? The Hebrew word for "devouring" in the scripture above is *bela* meaning to ruin or swallow up. What a way to describe the potential hidden in the power of the tongue.

A music teacher developed a soft spot for a talented student who sat at the back of his class. This bright teen was failing his class as a result of the negative words he choked down from his older brother. The student had planned to commit suicide, but a kind gesture from his music teacher altered his destiny.

The music teacher said, "You may not be performing well in my class, but I know you're brilliant. I'm giving you an A+ despite your low scores." And, that was the game-changer. The student went on to become the best in the class and grew up to have a beautiful family of his own. He would forever be grateful to his teacher for saving him with those life-building words.

How kind are your words? Stop slandering your so-called opponents. Embrace words of life and do away with destructive words. May the Lord bless you as you do this.

PRAYER

Father, it is written that the love of God has been shed abroad in our hearts as believers. Having received Your Holy Spirit and the fruit of the Spirit, I pray that gentle words be on my tongue and that I manifest kindness. I choose to build and not destroy others. I embrace words of life. I choose to stop allowing the enemy to use my mouth to hurt other people. In Jesus' name I pray. Amen.

THE FOOL'S PROVERB

As a thorn goeth up into the hands of a drunkard, so is a parable in the mouths of fools. (Proverbs 26:9)

Would you be comfortable sitting next to a drunk man who had sharp thorns protruding from his hands? Of course not! You would assume that given his current state, he could hurt you or even himself unintentionally. Words of "wisdom" in the mouth of a fool are just like thorns in the hands of a drunkard.

Some people love to joke about the Word of God or even make the things of God into curse words by adding Holy in front of any number of biblical names or anything else. They also take the name of our Lord in vain and use it with profanity. This type of foolish joking is likened to a drunkard's behavior. That's why you should not spend time listening to anything like that if you do not have to.

Do you joke with and about things you shouldn't? If so, God can clean you up from the inside out. Present yourself to Him today. He will teach you how to use your words wisely.

PRAYER

Dear God, please forgive me for any time I have joked with and about things I shouldn't have. Forgive me for the times I have taken the name of the Lord in vain. Please clean me up from the inside out. Lord, I pray that You will surround me with God-fearing people. Bless me with godly friends and keep me away from any bad influences. Keep profane people away from me. In Jesus' name I pray. Amen.

THE SIN OF
THOUGHTLESSNESS

Be not rash with thy mouth, and let not thine heart be
hasty to utter anything before God: for God is in heaven,
and thou upon earth: therefore let thy words be few.

(Ecclesiastes 5:2)

Spending time with the Lord is always wonderful. Consistent praise, worship, prayer and meditation in the Word of God strengthen the cords that bind us to Him. As a result, our hearts are filled with love, joy, and the peace of God.

God is passionate about spending time with us. He wants us to approach Him ready to listen and follow the leading of the Spirit of God. God pays detailed attention to all of our hearts' cries to Him.

We are often so enthusiastic that we can make promises that we cannot keep. We can also be so overwhelmed with our troubles that we make vows we cannot honour. Don't be so emotional that you commit yourself to anything outside of the will or Word of God.

When you appear before God, be calm and follow the direction of the Spirit of God while making your requests. Be thoughtful, listen, and do not be tempted to speak too many words.

PRAYER

Lord, when I come into Your presence, grant me the grace to be patient. Help me not to be wise with my words. Please forgive me for any vows and promises I did not keep or fulfil. I ask for mercy and pray that You will deliver me from any negative consequences emanating from my failure to fulfil any vows and promises made. In Jesus' name I pray. Amen.

YE ARE NOT
OF THE WORLD

They are of the world: therefore speak they of the world,
and the world heareth them. (1 John 4:5)

John spoke about the false teachers who do not have the knowledge of God. He said they deceive the hearts of men in subtle ways. As a guide to prevent us from falling into the hands of men with false doctrines, John describes the way and manner we can snuff them out.

The world is defined as anything different or contrary to the things of God. Worldly people neither know or understand the truth. They speak from a perspective that is contrary to the Word of God.

As a person saved from a sinful nature and called out from the world to become citizens of the Kingdom of God, your conversation must be different than that of the world. The Spirit of God who lives in you must be seen through your words and actions.

Speak of the things of God that build others up. Those who have the same spirit of God as you will acknowledge you. Do not be dejected when you are not accepted by certain people because they don't understand the things of God. Rather, through the daily confessions of the Word of God, you can use your words to draw others to Him. You are not of the world but of God. Let divine words proceed from your mouth.

PRAYER

Lord, I pray for the boldness to speak of the things of God that will build others up. Let me not be ashamed of the gospel for it is the power of God unto salvation to them that are perishing. May I stop conforming to the pattern of this world but be transformed in knowledge by the renewing of my mind. Let this mind which was in Christ Jesus be also in me to think, speak and act like You would, Lord. In Jesus' name I pray. Amen.

YOUR CONVERSATION

That ye put off concerning the former conversation the old man, which is corrupt according to the deceitful lust. (Ephesians 4:22)

I n a letter to the church in Ephesus, Paul admonishes believers to put away their former *conversation*. Amazingly, conduct was referred to as a *conversation*. I believe this means the way we speak has much to do with the kind of life we live.

> *The tongue also is a fire, a world of evil among the parts of the body. It corrupts the whole body, sets the whole course of one's life on fire, and is itself set on fire by hell.* (James 3:6, NIV)

We can deduce here that the mouth houses the *world of iniquity*. That's more reason for Paul to refer to our conduct as *conversation* according to the King James Version of the Bible.

To live a life free from ungodly conversation, it is essential to put off the old self, which is the sinful nature. This means we must die to sin through the holiness salvation provides. We can live free from corrupt conversation by filling up with the Word of God so that it spills out of our mouths instead of corruption.

PRAYER

Lord, help me crucify the flesh and die to sin through the holiness salvation provides. Help me to put off the old self, which is the sinful nature. Lord, please help me walk by the Spirit, that I may not gratify the desires of the old man nor the flesh. Let me be filled with the Word of God so that it may spill out of my mouth instead of corruption. In Jesus' name I pray. Amen.

LIVING SPRING
OF BLESSINGS

Out of the same mouth proceedeth blessing and cursing. My brethren, these things ought not so to be.

(James 3:10)

Have you ever seen a fountain that flows with both pure *and* filthy water? Of course not. Likewise, in the use of our tongues, it's unnatural to bless and curse at the same time.

Our moods determine what we say. Whatever is in us comes out of our mouths. When we are happy with them, we bless people. But when people annoy us, if we are not careful, we can use our mouths to speak curses and destruction. God's children must not live that way. We must subject our emotions to the Holy Spirit and keep our words in check. He will then show and teach us what to say even when our emotions want to act out.

Moreover, if our bodies are the temples of God, our mouths are the speakers of the temples. You won't hear chants to Baal and other false gods in Solomon's holy temple; in like manner, should we ever hear hurtful or sinful words from God's own temple? Never. The sound of the holy temple—words of our mouths—should be full of praises to God at all times: in the morning and at night, in good times and at bad times, when we are provoked and when we are at peace.

PRAYER

Lord, I submit my emotions to the Holy Spirit that I may obtain help to keep my words in check. Spirit of God, please show me and teach me what to say even when my emotions want to act out. May I cease to be a fountain that flows with filthy water. By Your grace and enablement may I be a living spring of blessings and advance the kingdom of God. In Jesus' name I pray. Amen.

WHAT DO YOU FEED ON?

The heart of him that hath understanding seeketh knowledge, but the mouth of fools feedeth on foolishness. (Proverbs 15:14)

Those who have understanding will diligently seek to be wise and truly desire knowledge. The unwise will neither desire to know Christ nor love the truth. Instead, they will be content with their present degree of knowledge.

A man of understanding will meditate and feed on God's Word. He will seek Him daily through prayer and study. But fools feed on things that tear down and waste time.

What you feed on will determine your heart's condition. The condition of your heart will determine your appetite—what you crave, prefer and enjoy. If you feed on God's Word, you will become wise. On the other hand, if you open your mind and heart to things that corrupt and pervert, you will become unwise. In turn, what you've fed on and are full of, is what will flow from your lips. Therefore, someone who seeks knowledge will speak edifying words, whereas someone who despises wise counsel will speak unwise words.

Clearly, if you desire to watch your mouth, you must watch what you feed on.

PRAYER

Heavenly Father, please give me an understanding heart. Lord, cause me to seek You like one would search for hidden treasure. May I be like the righteous man in Psalm 1. His delight is in the law of the Lord and in His law does he meditate day and night. Let me be like that tree planted by the rivers of water. As the deer pants for water let my soul long for You. Even as man shall not live by bread alone but every Word that proceeds from the mouth of God so let me thirst and hunger for Your Word. In Jesus' name I pray. Amen.

BLESS YOUR NATION

*By the blessing of the upright the city is exalted:
but it is overthrown by the mouth of the wicked.*

(Proverbs 11:11)

The United States of America is the world's leading superpower and influences other nations. The rise of the U.S. nation began with the emergence of great leaders, iconic industrialists, and innovative entrepreneurs. We would not be wrong if we said that it was also built on the pillars of prayer.

Americans have prayed "God bless America" for centuries. The streams of prayers coming from every corner of the country contributed to the vast development the United States is experiencing today. The phrase "God bless America" stemmed from a patriotic song composed by Irvin Berlin in 1918 during World War I. It has become a foundation of American culture.

> Then the Lord reached out his hand and touched my mouth and said to me, "I have put my words in your mouth. See, today I appoint you over nations and king-doms to uproot and tear down, to destroy and over-throw, to build and to plant." (Jeremiah 1:9-10, NIV)

Miracles happen when you pray for and say positive things about your country. A prayerful tongue creates wonderful things. Instead of castigating leaders for their errors, pray for them. By your blessings, your city will be lifted.

But negative words spoken by an unwise person can ruin a nation. Yet, when a righteous person speaks with authority, a broken nation can be rebuilt.

How often do you bless your nation? Do you want to see prosperity everywhere you look? Then keep professing great things about your nation and your family.

PRAYER

Dear God, please give me a burden to intercede for my nation, the body of Christ and the lost at large. Put Your words in my mouth to bless my nation and call forth Your purpose and plans in our cities and communities. By my words may I tear down, destroy and overthrow the kingdom of Satan and build and plant what is in Your will for my nation. In Jesus' name I pray. Amen.

JUST A SPARK

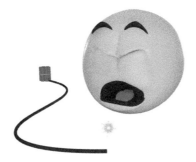

Even so the tongue is a little member, and boasteth great things. Behold, how great a matter a little fire kindleth! (James 3:5)

I n 1871, America experienced one of the greatest losses of all time. The great Chicago fire consumed properties worth $222 million at the time, killed 300 people, and left over 100,000 others homeless. Though the cause of the fire is still unknown, it's safe to assume that it started as a spark somehow, somewhere in the world's fastest-growing city at the time—Chicago.

> *In the same sense, the tongue is a small part of the body; yet, it boasts of great things. See [by comparison] how great a forest is set on fire by a small spark!*
> (James 3:5, AMP).

Just like the bit in the horse's mouth and the rudder of a mighty ship so is the tongue. It is tiny but powerful enough to dictate directions and conditions for something massively larger.

The tongue, like fire, can be handy when used correctly in Christian conversation. It brings warmth, encouragement, and grace to the hearers. Scriptures break open; hearts are set ablaze for God, and mighty miracles happen. But as fire should be carefully monitored to prevent uncontrolled destruction, so should men take heed, ensuring their words do not set others on fire in a negative way.

PRAYER

Dear God, I commit my tongue to glorify and to honor You. I commit my tongue to constructive and refreshing conversations. I decree and declare that my tongue is consecrated and anointed for godly purposes. My tongue shall not be used by the enemy to achieve his evil purposes. I declare that my tongue shall be a weapon of destruction in the hands of the Lord to destroy Satan's work and to advance God's Kingdom. Let many be encouraged and brought back to God through me as You put Your words in my mouth as You've promised. (Deuteronomy 18:18)

AUTHENTIC RELIGION

If any man among you seem to be religious, and bridles not his tongue, but deceives his own heart, this man's religion is in vain. (James 1:26, AKJV)

Self-control is a hallmark of any true Christian. It is the ability to regulate one's emotions, thoughts, and behaviors in the face of temptations and impulse. Self-control is a cognitive process that is necessary for governing one's behavior in order to achieve specific goals.

If you've mastered self-control, you know how to control or bridle your tongue. Not filtering what is coming out of your mouth has terrible consequences. Some find themselves in prison because they fail to bridle their tongues. All sorts of calamities have befallen many people because they could not control themselves.

Many have fallen into sin because of the words they have spoken.

> *In the multitude of words sin is not lacking, but he who restrains his lips is wise.* (Proverbs 10:19, NKJV)

You can't say everything you think. Let the Spirit of God be your guide on what to say, where, and when to say it.

Trying to defend and justify yourself may lead to unnecessary arguments. When your "yes" is "yes" and your "no" is "no", you won't expose yourself to strife which can lead to sin.

Are you too talkative? Learn to exercise self-control. Never allow your emotions or pride to lead your conversations. Control your tongue.

PRAYER

Lord, I pray for the grace to exercise self-control. I ask for the wisdom to know what to say and what not to say. Grant me the understanding to know the appropriate time to speak when necessary. May my words be few for in the multitude of words sin is not lacking. May I not be led by my flesh, but instead, influenced by the fruit of the Holy Spirit in me. Deliver me from unnecessary and unprofitable arguments. I place my thoughts and emotions under Your control. In Jesus' name I pray. Amen.

THINK BEFORE YOU SPEAK

The heart of the righteous studieth to answer: but the mouth of the wicked poureth out evil things.

(Proverbs 15:28)

A righteous man chooses his words carefully. He considers and weighs his words before releasing them because his words build or destroy.

As a believer, you must not be quick to give answers. Allow the Spirit of God to guide your thoughts and tongue. You are God's representative on earth, so it's important to utter words that will glorify the Lord whom you represent.

Many people listen only enough to give a reply. They do not care if what proceeds from their mouths are seasoned words and that are right for the moment. Instead, they let their emotions, whether anger, hatred, or frustration direct their speech. However, it should not be the same for a believer. You are called to speak words of hope, truth, and life.

Think carefully before you speak on any matter. Because what you speak will be what you see, ultimately. Do your words stir up or turn away strife? Do they build people up or break them down? Think about the possible effect of your words on people before you speak.

PRAYER

Father, I pray for the grace to be quick to listen and slow to speak. Grant me the grace to choose carefully my words weighing them before releasing them. Help me to remember that words have consequences. Please help me to speak with the desired outcome at the forefront of my mind. Grant that I will be influenced by You whenever I speak. May I never speak from a negative emotional standpoint, to harm, to hurt, or to destroy in any way. Lord, answer these prayers and many more that I haven't asked in this regard. In Jesus' name I pray. Amen.

WHAT FILLS
YOUR MOUTH?

Whose mouth is full of cursing and bitterness.

(Romans 3:14)

Have you ever seen a cup full of water but overflowing with milk? A cup full of water will overflow with water, and a cup full of milk will overflow with milk. Likewise, our mouths dispense what we are filled with on the inside.

What words spill out of your mouth when you speak? The words you utter well up from the knowledge you possess, whether it's good or bad.

*A good man out of the good treasure of his heart brings
forth good; and an evil man out of the evil treasure of*

his heart brings forth evil. For out of the abundance of the heart, the mouth speaks. (Luke 6:45, NIV)

Do you speak negative words at the slightest provocation, or do you stand strong in faith, releasing words of affirmation in the most frustrating situations? It all depends on what's in you. Every fruit (word) of your mouth has deep roots in your heart.

Therefore, it is vital to supervise what enters your heart. Take note of the information you let in because it will pop right out as soon as you open your mouth! But the good news is, you can fill your heart with good things. You can make positive declarations, express faith in challenging times, and call good things into your life when you first carry them in your heart.

PRAYER

Heavenly Father, I thank You for being my Father and King. Lord, fill my mouth with Your Word. By the influence of Your Spirit in my mouth I speak strength to my soul. I speak blessing on my family, community, ministry and business. I speak progress over my church. I speak advancement over my nation. No matter what the situation is, let me understand exactly what to say. In Jesus' name I pray. Amen.

THE SIN OF MURMURING

These are murmurers, complainers, walking after their own lusts; and their mouth speaketh great swelling words, having men's persons in admiration because of advantage. (Jude 1:16)

God is love!

For God so loved the world, that he gave his only begotten Son, that whosoever believeth in him should not perish, but have everlasting life. (John 3:16)

The Bible says God so loved the "world" and that includes everyone. What are you going through which makes you turn your back to this great love?

You may be undergoing a major challenge or setback, causing you to use your tongue in an unproductive way—murmuring and complaining. Have you turned away from God by chasing your own lust? Is your mouth speaking negative words because of disappointment, hurt, and pain?

Know that God's love still abounds toward you. The truth is, complaining and murmuring will not bring you answers from God. It doesn't change your circumstance and only makes it worse. On the other hand, offering thanksgiving and expressing gratitude to God will encourage Him to work things out in your favor. Usher in God's love with the right words and quit complaining.

God loves you dearly and will supply your needs according to the riches of His glory! Stay positive; speak rightly and watch God work things out on your behalf, more than you can imagine or think.

PRAYER

Heavenly Father, I thank You for Your Word. Dear Lord, please forgive me for anytime I have murmured and complained. I sincerely repent and ask for the grace to trust You in all circumstances. Help me to be grateful. Your Word declares that there is no fear or uncertainty in love. Therefore, I choose to trust in Your love. I will bless You at all times and Your praise will continually be in my mouth. In Jesus' name I pray. Amen.

POISONOUS TONGUE

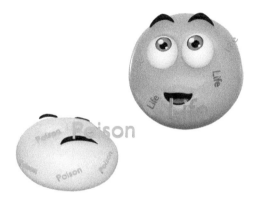

*But the tongue can no man tame, it is an unruly evil
full of deadly poison.* (James 3:8)

The tongue is a soft, movable part of the mouth that has caused the downfall of many mighty men who resisted taming it. Equally, amazing feats have been accomplished by the most unlikely men using this same weapon. You can build a wonderful life or a tragic life by the way you use your tongue.

Your tongue can act as a deadly instrument when you continuously pronounce evil things over your life, family, ministry, or education. Such a subtle instrument is delicate and should be treated with extreme care. The Bible says, *But the tongue can no man tame.* It doesn't matter how smart you are or how many degrees you have.

The Holy Spirit helps you harness this powerful body part, to speak life instead of death, blessings instead of curses, and hope instead of despair. By speaking and meditating on God's Word, you neutralize the potential for poison inherent in your tongue.

Every individual has a choice—a choice to *Yield yourselves unto God, as those alive from the dead, and your members as instruments of righteousness unto God* (Romans 6:13) or to do the opposite. Your choice determines your results in life. Fill your heart and mind with God's Word and your conversation shall be a blessing to you and everyone around you.

PRAYER

Father, thank You for Your Word. I dedicate my tongue to You for positive use to advance Your cause. Instead of poison, it will utter life. Instead of destruction, it will construct and be a permanent channel of blessings. Furthermore, may it be a source of inspiration to all those who hear me. This I pray, in the name that is superior to every other name, Jesus-Christ of Nazareth, Son of the living God. Amen.

DAY

32

NO FILTHY CONVERSATION

But now ye also put off all these; anger, wrath, malice, blasphemy, filthy communication out of your mouth.

(Colossians 3:8)

After you were redeemed from your lifestyle of sin, you were called to exhibit the righteousness of God, which is Christ Jesus. Your mind has been renewed from the works of the flesh. And you are now called to walk in the fullness of life and righteousness.

You are not saved to go on living carelessly. Instead, God gives you His Spirit to guide your conduct. God is interested in the way you use your tongue as you live in your renewed state. He wants you to put off the old way of living, including your old vocabulary. He classifies every word you utter in anger and hate, every blasphemous and malicious phrase, and all unwholesome talk as sin.

More than that, He wants you to take on a new form of conversation, *And put on the new man* (Colossians 3:10). God wants you to speak pure words that represent your new status in Christ. He wants you to substitute truth for lies, love for hate, blessings for curses, and faith for doubt.

Try to do away with words that don't edify. Refrain from using words that foster disunity among the people of God. The liberty God gave you in the new birth is not a license to live a haphazard life. As a believer, the words of your mouth must be full of grace, seasoned with salt, and capable of giving strength to the depressed.

PRAYER

Abba Father, I thank You for Your precious Word today. Lord, I pray for the grace to walk in newness of life. I put off the old man and put on the new man which is renewed after the image of Christ. As I put away my old way of living, including my old vocabulary, I pray for the grace to substitute truth for lies, love for hate, blessings for curses, and faith for doubt. May this new image in Christ continue to be a living testimony and serve as a living epistle to all. In Jesus' name I pray. Amen.

NO CORRUPT COMMUNICATION

Let no corrupt communication proceeds out of your mouth, but that which is good to use of edifying, that it may minister grace unto the hearer. (Ephesians 4:29)

Imagine a student who just failed an exam having his friend come over. Of course, he is dejected and hopes to be comforted. Unfortunately, his expectations are flushed down the drain when his friend ridicules and embarrasses him. He spits out words of discouragement and hopelessness that cause depression.

The point is corrupt conversation has devastating effects. Corrupt communication flows from a corrupt heart.

Out of the abundance of the heart, the mouth speaks.

(Luke 6:45, NIV)

Friend, pay attention to the words that proceed out of your mouth. God wants your words to encourage, enlighten, comfort, and heal the brokenhearted. Paul said to speak "to one another with psalms, hymns, and songs from the Spirit" (Ephesians 5:19, NIV). So, speak to uplift and inspire the hearts of your listeners. You create your world with your words, so stay away from corrupt discussions.

PRAYER

Precious Lord, I am grateful for Your Word once again. Let my words be seasoned with salt and light. Let them carry strength and convey faith in You and respect towards humanity. Whether in psalms, hymns, or melodies, may I speak words that encourage, enlighten, comfort, and heal the brokenhearted. Out of the abundance of the heart, the mouth speaks. Therefore, I pray that my heart and mind be filled with godly thoughts to meditate on whatever is true, noble, right, pure, lovely, admirable, excellent or worthy of praise. In Jesus' name I pray. Amen.

CONTENTMENT IN CONVERSATION

Let your conversation be without covetousness; and be content with such things as ye have: for he hath said, I will never leave thee, nor forsake thee. (Hebrews 13:5)

To covet is to feel inordinate desire for what belongs to another person. Have you ever seen someone who is always talking about someone else's property or success and wishing to have it? What about people who always complain about their own lives? These people do not express contentment in their conversations. Their covetousness is revealed by their words.

Let your speech reflect contentment and gratitude toward God. Channel your heartfelt affection to God all the days of your life. Surely, you will never lack anything good in life. Be sure that your interactions with people reflect peace and confidence in God.

If you are not satisfied with what you have in life, go to God and find out what He has in store for you when you follow His plan for your life. He is a good father who wants what's best for all of His children. What He has for you is for you. Knowing this keeps you from longing for what someone else has.

God wants us to be wise enough to acknowledge Him as God, the great and impartial provider. He wants us to be content and appreciative of what He has given unto us. Talk about your trust in God and your gratitude for what He has given you.

PRAYER

Dear Lord, please teach my heart to be content with what I have while waiting for other blessings and promotions from You. Help me not to envy nor compare myself to others. Help me count my blessings and name them one by one. Teach me also to be grateful for what I already have, knowing that my God shall supply all my needs according to His riches in glory through Christ Jesus. Lord, please grant me the grace to trust You wholeheartedly with all the issues of my life, knowing that I can always depend on You. In Jesus' name I pray. Amen.

DON'T SPEAK WITHOUT UNDERSTANDING

But these, as natural brute beasts, made to be taken and destroyed, speak evil of the things that they understand not; and shall utterly perish in their own corruption.

(2 Peter 2:12)

What is the common characteristic of beasts? It's is their primitive minds and behavior. So for the scriptures to compare someone to a beast, it means the person has descended below human nature. These are people the Bible calls unjust, *them that walk after the flesh in the lust of uncleanness* (2 Peter 2:10).

The mouth is supposed to speak from a wealth of understanding, but brute beasts speak against things they know little or nothing about. They are arrogant and lack good judgment. For instance, some people openly proclaim that there is no God when they can't logically explain their existence.

But God's children are not beasts and are expected to show reverence in their conversations. Your words should reveal honor for sacred things and humility concerning spiritual matters. In fact, the Bible says...

> For the invisible things of him from the creation of the world are clearly seen, being understood by the things that are made, even his eternal power and Godhead; so that they are without excuse. (Romans 1:20)

The more you honor the things of God, the more God honors you. Stay humble. Let God guide your lips that His blessings may rest upon you.

PRAYER

Lord, I pray for the wisdom to not to speak about things which I know nothing about. I pray for the grace to keep quiet when I need to and never to open my mouth hastily to speak about things I do not understand. Lord, please protect my heart from pride. May I always remain teachable, available, and quick to make the necessary adjustments to help me be a better person. In Jesus' name I pray. Amen.

SPEAK WELL OF
DIGNITARIES

Honor

But chiefly them that walk after the flesh in the lust of uncleanness, and despise government. Presumptuous are they, self-willed, they are not afraid to speak evil of dignities. (2 Peter 2:10)

The situation and the people involved determine the choice of word use. The English language continues to expand, yet, the 20-volume *Oxford English Dictionary* (2ⁿᵈ Edition) has over 171,000 words in use. Of these words, some are unto life, while others are unto death. Also, certain combinations could either be fatal or miraculous.

As the occasion demands, we must be careful to select our words based on whom we are dealing with. In the text above, apostle Peter points to a certain set of rebels and wrongdoers. Moreover, they are fearless when they stand before prominent members of society.

Do not be presumptuous while standing before dignitaries. Be bold and articulate, but also humble and respectful in your speech. Be careful how you speak against those in authority. Always let your speech be seasoned with grace, so that you may know how to answer every man (Colossians 4:8).

PRAYER

Dear Lord, thank You for Your Word. I pray that You will teach me, by revelation, how to best deal with dignitaries. Lord, I pray that I will not run my mouth unnecessarily in these situations as a result of ignorance or zeal. May my speech be seasoned with grace, so that I may know how to answer every man. Help me to be bold, articulate, humble, and respectful – giving honor to whom it is due. In Jesus' name I pray. Amen.

NEW BIRTH RESPONSIBILITIES

Therefore, if anyone is in the Messiah, he is a new creation. Old things have disappeared, and—look!—all things have become new! (2 Corinthians 5:17, ISV)

The new birth is a mystery that is yet to be understood by many. Even some believers are still mystified by the amazing possibilities that come with the experience of the new birth in Christ Jesus through the Holy Spirit. One remarkable attribute of the new birth is newness of life.

As beautiful as this experience is, this new nature is first resident in your spirit before it is expressed outwardly. Before you were born again, your soul had ample opportunity to gather junk.

Therefore, when you are born again, it is your responsibility to renew your mind and start emptying the trash.

You must get rid of bitterness, hate, envy, fear, and profanity from your old life. If you don't make a concerted effort to renew your mind, as well as your tongue, you will discover yourself repeating old negative cycles. This means you have to resolve that whatever belongs to the old man will no longer be a part of your new life in Christ. Your tongue has to be divinely reconfigured to speak good things.

Dedicate time toward studying God's Word. Pray without ceasing asking God to reshape your life. He will grant your requests, and you'll begin to grow into His image. By the power of the cross, your sinful nature will give way to your renewed spirit-man, and great shall be your transformation and testimony.

PRAYER

King of glory, I appreciate You for Your Word. I am a new creature in You. Old things have passed away and all things have become new! Let my new position in You be the basis for my living. Grant me grace and understanding to represent Christ in all things I do and say. May the flesh and the old man not have dominion over me. May I have the upper hand to be victorious. In Jesus' name I pray. Amen.

RESPECTFUL IN WORDS

Likewise also these filthy dreamers defile the flesh,
despise dominion, and speak evil of dignities. (Jude 1:8)

Angels are creatures that stand before God's throne and carry out His commands. They are beings of glory and light that represent God Himself. There are different kinds of angels and among them are the cherubim who are symbols of God's holiness.

In the above text, Jude doesn't talk about earthly kings and dignitaries but beings and saints that hold rank in the kingdom of God.

Because of the role they play in God's agenda and government, these supernatural beings are to be respected. They are ambassadors of the sovereign Lord and communicators of His dominion. But there are those who speak against and curse heavenly messengers and God's servants on the earth.

Jude warns us not to be part of those who speak lies to satisfy their desires. Such people are insolent and disrespectful. They despise God and heavenly beings and scoff at dignitaries. Stay true to the faith handed down to us from our fathers of the faith. Always show respect in word and attitude toward those who deserve it.

PRAYER

Lord, I bless You today and thank You for Your words of life. Lord I pray for the grace to honor and respect sacred systems and institutions. Grant me revelation when certain authorities were ordained by God and carry dimensions for advancement. Let me now trivialize godly principles. It is in the name of Jesus that I pray with thanksgiving. Amen.

LESSONS FROM FALSE TEACHERS

For when they speak great swelling words of vanity,
they allure through the lusts of the flesh, through much
wantonness, those that were clean escaped from them
who live in error. (2 Peter 2:18)

Have you heard words that inspire you to dream? What about encouraging words that move you to tears and set your heart on fire? Did those words lead you to your heavenly Father? Or did they take you further away from Him?

The world is filled with many preachers and teachers who have exchanged sound doctrine for error. Peter makes us realize that they speak great swelling words of vanity. These are teachers who are not spiritually led but intellectually driven and attach importance to vain imaginations. They appear to bring illumination, but their purpose is to glorify themselves.

As followers of Christ, God wants us to distinguish ourselves from such people. We must speak the truth and live by what we proclaim. Indeed, only the truth can deliver hearts from bondage and transform from darkness to light. Consequently, our words must not gratify the flesh. Rather, the words of our mouths must be full of the spirit and life. They must strengthen the hearers to perform and become what they say.

Moreover, God desires us to be conformed to the image of His dear Son Jesus. When Jesus was on the earth, He taught the undiluted truth of God's Word. And Jesus had this testimony: He practiced His doctrine before teaching it.

Therefore, His lifestyle and conduct showed the authenticity and power of His message. Indeed, we can say that Jesus only said what He did. Think about it for a moment. If we only say what we practice, then it'll be difficult to teach what is false or deceptive.

Do you ask people to live by ridiculous standards you can't live up to yourself? Take a U-turn by walking the talk. Don't desire to speak mere inflated words; aim to influence lives with practical truth that leads to righteous and godly living.

PRAYER

Lord, I praise You and bless You today for Your wonderful Word. Dear Father, I pray for the grace to be a pragmatic child of God, being a doer of the Word and not just a mere listener. I pray for the grace to live up to Your expectations. Grant that by the application of the keys of the kingdom, the whole counsel of God will become my practical experience. Let me fulfil the will of God and advance His kingdom. In Jesus' name I pray. Amen.

PUT IT AWAY

Let all bitterness, and wrath, and anger, and clamour, and
evil speaking, be put away from you, with all malice.

(Ephesians 4:31)

The Bible instructs believers to renew our minds and present our bodies as living sacrifices to God. We are also told to build up ourselves in our most holy faith praying in the Holy Ghost (Jude 1:20). However, our spirits, minds, and bodies are not the only parts of us that need some exercise. The scripture above tells us what to do with our mouths: keep evil speaking as far from them as possible.

If we've been born of God's Spirit, we need to renew our minds and change the way we formerly did things. This includes the words we speak to ourselves and others. In fact, God gives us full responsibility for what comes out of our mouths by saying, "Put way from you." That's a clear indication that we all need to overcome the bad habit of speaking negative words. We have the power to choose how we speak and can exercise discipline in areas of weakness.

Indeed, speaking wholesome words as a believer is a responsibility God will hold you accountable for. So, it's important to put away everything that makes you sin against God by always saying positive, faith-filled words.

PRAYER

Lord, I exalt You and bless You today for Your precious Word. Father, I receive the grace and ability to put away from me all bitterness, wrath, anger, clamor, and evil speaking, with all malice. Lord, please let Your love fill my heart. I release and forgive anyone who has offended me. I let go of negative situations. Make me a vessel of mercy so that I can obtain mercy. Help me to keep moving forward. Help me to always watch my mouth. In Jesus' name I pray. Amen.

OTHER BOOKS
BY EDDIE

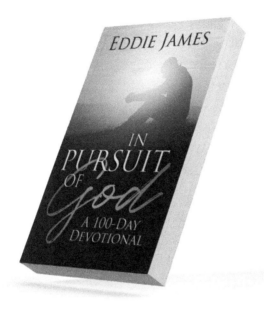

In Pursuit of God
A 100-Day Devotional

M oment by moment, we have choices to make, people to meet, battles to fight, temptations to resist, and relationships to build. These are all integral parts of our world. Here and there, we experience fear, anxiety, doubts, and even lose faith. How we navigate this maze of daily living and earthly struggles will determine the quality of our lives now and tomorrow.

This 100-Day devotional is a practical guide designed to help you walk the walk and succeed. It's loaded with encouragement, wisdom, prayers, and the Word of God to empower you on life's journey. In just a few minutes each day, you will spend quality moments with God studying His life-transforming Word. Each devotional gets straight to the heart of the matter and will help you grow in faith and intimacy with God.

If you want to improve your life and build better relationships, here is a good place to start. Take some time each day to focus on what God says in His Word. Gain the encouragement, guidance, and clarity you need. It will keep you surefooted and wise on your path to right living.

ISBN 9781562293994 Paperback | ISBN 9781562295066 eBook

Available wherever books are sold and
from ChristianLivingBooks.com

ABOUT THE AUTHOR

E ddie James is a worship artist, minister, and founder of Eddie James Ministries, Eddie James Productions, DreamLife, Fresh Wine Records, and Fresh Wine Publishing. He is the Associate Pastor and Worship Director for Nations Church in Orlando, FL (Daniel Kolenda, Pastor). He has been in ministry for more than 30 years and traveled full time for 18 years.

As an internationally renowned worship artist, he releases his songs of worship to many of the world's most impactful ministries. These ministries include Daniel Kolenda, Bishop T.D. Jakes, Lou Engle, The Call, Bill Johnson, Bethel Music, Perry Stone, Karen Wheaton, Kirk Franklin, and many more. His song wrtiing, production, and artistry have carried his music to the top of the Billboard Charts. "I Am," "Lord, You're Holy," "Psalm 23," "You've Been So Faithful," "Breakthrough," and "Freedom" are just a few of the songs for which he is known.

His songs have been performed by a wide range of music artists and ministries, from Judy Jacobs, Karen Wheaton and Helen Baylor to Lakeland Church, Brooklyn Tabernacle, and Mississippi Mass Choir. His works have been featured on Fox News, Glen Beck, Oprah Winfrey Network and "Lion of Judah" produced by Warner Brothers. His music and sound are sought around the world, evidenced by his appearances on TBN, God-TV, Daystar, "Sid Roth's It's Supernatural" and in magazines like "Charisma."

Eddie rescues, restores, and raises high school and college-age youth who are coming out of drug addiction, street life, gangs, violence, abuse, and perverse lifestyles through a recovery program known as DreamLife Ministries. When he is not traveling, he is with his spiritual and adopted sons and daughters, teaching his discipleship program called "Discipleship N Arts" (DNA). Hundreds of youths have been empowered to experience a life of freedom and discover their true significance. Many of them now have ministries of their own or are serving in powerful ministries and churches.

Let's Stay Connected

Connect with Us: eddiejames.com

Connect with Us: dreamlifecenters.com

Find/Follow Us: Instagram: eddiejames_

Find/Follow Us: Facebook: Eddie James (Official)

Find/Follow Us: Twitter: ejworship

Watch Us: eddiejames.tv

Download Us: freshwinemusic.com

Pray 4 Us: In Jesus' name